Personal Quiet Time

Brief words of meditation on Christ's
suffering, death and resurrection to help give
people hope in their lives.

Verna Rudolph

OPENBOOK
PUBLISHERS

OPENBOOK
PUBLISHERS

Copyright © 1989

The Bible quotations appearing here are from the *New
International Version*, © 1978 the New York International Bible
Society.

Cover photograph: Sam Zarember — The Image Bank.

First printing July 1989

00 99 98 97   10 9 8 7 6 5

National Library of Australia
Cataloguing-in-Publication entry

Rudolph, Verna.
    Personal quiet time.

    ISBN 0 85910 516 4.

    1. Jesus Christ – Passion – Meditations.
    2. Jesus Christ – Crucifixion – Meditations.
    3. Jesus Christ – Resurrection – Meditations.
    I. Title

242'.5

Openbook Publishers
205 Halifax Street, Adelaide, South Australia   1503-95

We need to take time occasionally for
contemplation —
a quiet time to reappraise our lives;
a stocktaking for all of us to do on our own
lives —
and we find that we have fallen short.

I need such a time to 'take refuge' —
to be apart from the outside world;
to reminisce about my own life, about
'myself';
to take stock of my life's directions;
to gather strength to go back into the
world again.

The Christian church, in the traditional Church
Year, has provided such a period for each
year. It is called Lent and Easter, and is a
time when we remember Jesus' suffering,
death and resurrection, and what they
mean for us personally.

Lord, bless my efforts to sort myself out. Amen.

Let not the wise man boast of his wisdom or the strong man boast of his strength or the rich man boast of his riches, but let him who boasts boast about this: that he understands and knows me, that I am the Lord (Jer. 9:23,24).

Each of us is called on to know the Lord —
in an intimate personal relationship, as in a marriage.

St Paul says: 'Work out your salvation with fear and trembling' (Phil. 2:12) —
not in our own actions or good works,
but in contemplation and growth, in repentance and knowledge —
'for it is God who works in you'.

We must know the Lord in faith, so that we can live continually as servants of God,
shedding his light in this dark world,
showing his love and forgiveness to all sinners.

To be able to do this, we need to spend time alone with our Mentor and Friend.

During the season of Lent, and at any time, we can come and spend time in the refuge of God's everlasting arms.

Rend your heart and not your garments. Return to the Lord your God, for he is gracious and compassionate, slow to anger and abounding in love (Joel 2:13).

We all feel guilt at times —
    our sins weigh us down,
    our life seems meaningless,
    our work, our life, and the endless grind
    seem to have no point.

Our inner self tells us to rely on God —
    to call on him for the answers,
    to acknowledge that he is our only refuge.

So we spend time with God —
    quietly,
    reflectively,
    honestly.

And to all those who come to him, he gives
    blessing —
    his steadfast love,
    his unmerited mercy,
    his complete forgiveness.

Though your sins are like scarlet, they shall be as white as snow; though they are as red as crimson, they shall be like wool (Isa. 1:18).

Yes, we have fallen short of what God requires of us.
God requires something different from each of us,
but he requires that we do it perfectly.

Yes, we need to acknowledge this fact,
and the fact that we need help.
And God is the only one who can do this perfectly.

Yes, God has the answer —
he washes us clean, squeaky clean;
his washing is so perfect that it remains effective for ever.

Three cheers for God —
hooray,
hooray,
hooray!

Search me, O God, and know my heart; test me and know my anxious thoughts. See if there is any offensive way in me, and lead me in the way everlasting (Ps. 139:23,24).

God knows me — my every thought, my every move.

Now I need to know myself —
> to consider my words, to think about my actions;
> to be conscious of all that I do;
> to acknowledge that I am not perfect;
> to put into words my sins;
> to accept God's forgiveness for myself.

For I know that only God can lead me into heaven.

> *Lead thou me on, thou kindly, heavenly Light,*
> *lead thou me on;*
> *My pathway home is shrouded in dark night,*
> *I see no dawn.*
> *Thou art the light dispelling this world's gloom;*
> *light thou my path, and lead me safely home.*

He will call upon me, and I will answer him; I will be with him in trouble, I will deliver him and honour him. With long life will I satisfy him and show him my salvation (Ps. 91:15,16).

There are 40 days in Lent, excluding the Sundays. Traditionally the Sundays have not been counted because all Sundays are celebrations of the resurrection.

The resurrection was God's ultimate, perfect answer to our call for help. God not only solves our BIG problem — sin. He also answers all our calls for help, including all the little troubles and crises of every day, for all people, in all the world.

So on Sundays we celebrate — and on weekdays we contemplate.

The vertex — and the vortex — of our contemplation and celebration are Jesus' suffering, death, and resurrection.

'The multitude of your sacrifices — what are they to me?' says the Lord. 'I have more than enough of burnt offerings, of rams and the fat of fattened animals; I have no pleasure in the blood of bulls and lambs and goats' (Isa. 1:11).

Sacrifices —
  were needed to wipe out the sin of the
    people;
  were offered to make atonement for a
    person (Lev. 1:4);
  were an outward act, symbolic of an
    inward repentance.

Sacrifices are like pious words, worthy actions,
    extra church services — something we
    can all do very easily.

But God is not impressed with outward actions.

He does not want external things —
    he wants hearts and lives and people.

*Take my life and let it be
consecrated, Lord, to thee.*

Wash and make yourselves clean. Take your evil deeds out of my sight! Stop doing wrong, learn to do right! Seek justice, encourage the oppressed. Defend the cause of the fatherless, plead the case of the widow (Isa. 1:16,17).

The other prophets preach the same message. See Micah 6:8, Jeremiah 22:3, and Hosea 6:6.

God calls his people to follow his way. But he gives them a choice:

Choose money, prestige, power, self — and selfishness, greed, pride, gluttony will rule your life.
Or choose Me, and show steadfast love, do justice,
walk humbly with the Lord your God.

Be different,
be clean,
be Mine.

And I can do far more for you
than all the rest put together.

Here I am. Send me! (Isa. 6:8)

May the words of my mouth and the meditation of my heart be pleasing in your sight, O Lord, my Rock and my Redeemer (Ps. 19:14).

Whether you eat or drink or whatever you do, do it all for the glory of God (1 Cor. 10:31).

Every little thought,
     every big consideration,
     every feeling transformed into action,
     every act deliberately carried out,
     everything that I do, —
     may they all be to the glory of God.

God, forgive me when I fail;
     pick me up, dust me off,
     and give me the courage to try again.
     Amen.

Blessed is the man you discipline, O Lord, the man you teach from your law; you grant him relief from days of trouble (Ps. 94:12,13).

Trouble, depression, destruction, sickness, disasters —
> we think of them as curses in our lives;
> we think that they are sent to teach us a lesson;
> we reason that they are punishment for some sin of long ago.

The Psalmist considers them a blessing!

Laws, orders, directions, commandments —
> what a humbug they seem to be in our lives,
> binding us to what we have to do,
> restricting our fun and freedom.

The Psalmist considers them the way out of our troubles!

God's laws are a signpost pointing us away from the evil that is around us and in us. When we are thus facing God, we receive many blessings and much support from him (see Ps. 94:18).

Lord, forgive our backward thinking;
> *help us overcome our reverse attitudes;*
> *turn us 180° to your point of view. Amen.*

But you, O Sovereign Lord, deal well with me for your name's sake; out of the goodness of your love, deliver me. For I am poor and needy, and my heart is wounded within me (Ps. 109:21,22).

You deal well with me —
        for your name's sake;
        in your steadfast love.

God, you do everything for me from your point
        of view —
        not because of how good I am;
        not because I will be good in return;
but because you reach out to me in a caring
        love —
        not counting the cost;
        not expecting or forcing a response (but
            loving me when I do respond);
        not because you have to, but because you
            want to;
knowing that I will be happier when I do.

*Thank you for being you,
        for saving me;
        for Jesus' sake. Amen.*

God is our refuge and strength, an ever-present help in trouble (Ps. 46:1).

Trouble is sin, both specific and general;
it is disaster, storms, accidents;
it is ill-health, depression, death;
it is the experience of nothing turning out right.

God is the answer —
the lighthouse in the storm;
the rock on which to build (instead of sinking sand);
the light at the end of the tunnel;
the shoulder to cry on;
the fortress (with moat) which protects us in time of war;
the breakwater around a quiet harbour;
the punching bag to vent our anger on;
the hand that guides the blind and the helpless through traffic.

God, I need all these, all the time.
Continue to support me in my life. Amen.

The Lord is our judge; the Lord is our lawgiver;
the Lord is our king; it is he who will save us
(Isa. 33:22).

A football commentator was heard to say, after a deliberate and obvious infringement of one of the rules: 'O well, if you can get away with it, that's OK!'

Adam blamed Eve and God. Eve blamed the devil. We are no different — we also try to get out of being guilty. We want to be in the right, to be innocent.

In our western judicial system, we are considered innocent until proved guilty.

But God sees into our hearts; in his eyes we are guilty until we are made blameless — by Jesus!

God's justice condemns us.
God's love and mercy forgives us — because Jesus makes it happen.

Lord, thank you for forgiveness. It makes life worth living. Amen.

*Remember, O Lord, your great mercy and love,
for they are from of old. Remember not the sins
of my youth and my rebellious ways; according to
your love remember me, for you are good, O Lord
(Ps. 25:6,7).*

When the Bible speaks about remembering, it doesn't mean only an intellectual exercise of recalling events in the past; it also involves an emotional bond and a spiritual exercise. Remembering involves knowing that I came through the Red Sea with Moses and crossed the Jordan River with Joshua, and my feelings about it. These great deeds of God in the past have meaning for my life now, and I respond with praise, thanksgiving, and action dedicated to God.

We remember God —
    the Father who created us;
    the Son who died for us;
    the Spirit who washes us.

And God remembers us, too —
    by his work at Creation, Calvary, and
        Pentecost;
    by loving, forgiving, and supporting us;
    by giving us a home in heaven.

For to us a child is born, to us a son is given
(Isa. 9:6).

A baby ...
A baby is cuddly, cute, adorable, innocent!
A baby is non-threatening.
Everyone loves a baby —
it is easy to know what to do with a
baby.

A man ...
What now?
Ignore him? — with eternal consequences.
Accept him? — a traitor on a cross?
Befriend him? — only if he reciprocates!
Talk about him? — but nobody wants to
listen!
Love him? — with what kind of love?

Yes, what do we do with him now?

Lord,
help me still to adore the Son who gave his
life for me. Amen.

*He will be called Wonderful Counsellor, Mighty
God, Everlasting Father, Prince of Peace*
(Isa. 9:6).

Jesus was given earthly names, an earthly
job —
  the only terms we can understand are
    earthly terms;
  it was on earth that the work had to be
    done;
  it had to be done for earthly people, who
    wouldn't and couldn't make it to heaven
    by themselves;
  he had to be truly a man to fulfil the laws
    perfectly.

But —
  these names could only be applied to
    Someone from outside our world;
  his was a heavenly mission, coming from
    heaven to bring people to heaven;
  because he is the Son of God, the King of
    kings, the Lord of Lords.

Lord Jesus,
  your name tells us a lot about you.
  Help us to use it often. Amen.

Hear, O Lord, and answer me ... In the day of my
trouble I will call to you, for you will answer me
(Ps. 86:1,7).

It's good, in a conversation, to get an answer
to a question. (Having lived with someone who
doesn't always hear, I know that it can be
frustrating, confusing, and hard on a
relationship not to get an answer.)

God's answers always come. But they are not
necessarily the ones we want, so we don't
always hear them.

God's answer may be:
> yes;
> no;
> maybe something else;
> wait.

Which answer is it this time?

How will God's answer come? Will it be:
> the still, small voice?
> the thunder and lightning?
> the secret message?
> the public announcement? —
> Will I be sure it is from God?

Lord,
> *clean out my ears, my heart, my eyes, my*
> *mind, so that I can hear you. Amen.*

Before they call I will answer; while they are still speaking I will hear (Isa. 65:24).

Humanity's first encounter with sin, evil, doubt, pride, and temptation led to God's answer — the same answer that is given all through the Bible.

Adam and Eve, Noah, Abraham, Moses, and David all had the same need, and God's response was always ready for them.

Eventually Jesus came, and people could see and hear and experience the answer given to each of them personally.

Our need (as well as theirs) for forgiveness was answered on a cross outside Jerusalem.

Lord,
thank you for thinking of me so long ago.
Amen.

The Lord is gracious and compassionate, slow to anger and rich in love. The Lord is good to all; he has compassion on all he has made (Ps. 145:8,9).

The poor of India,
the hungry of Africa,
the suffering of South America,
the oppressed of Russia,
the wealthy of Europe,
the desperate of slums everywhere,
the lost and lonely,
the busy and the unemployed,
the sick, sorrowing, homeless, and handicapped —
all are loved, forgiven, fed, clothed, and befriended by God.

Lord,
help me to remember that I am one of many, and that I have enough to share with others — especially your Word. Amen.

*My eyes are ever on the Lord, for only he will
release my feet from the snare. Turn to me and be
gracious to me, for I am lonely and afflicted*
(Ps. 25:15,16).

Loneliness, shame, and rejection were
borne for our good.

A purpose, a direction, and grit were needed to
bring us salvation.

God knew that a servant — a suffering, lowly
worker — could do it all.

The prophet Isaiah wrote about the Servant of
the Lord. Whether these servant songs of
Isaiah originally referred to Isaiah himself,
the king, some other individual, or the
nation, is not so important any more.

They help us to see who our Suffering Servant
is now, and how he was meant to save us.

God,
because Jesus was lonely and afflicted,
you are gracious to me.
Thank you. Amen.

Here is my servant ... A bruised reed he will not
break, and a smouldering wick he will not snuff
out. In faithfulness he will bring forth justice
(Isa 42:1,3).

Human responses to God and his Word
include scoffing, laughing, and unbelief.
These often have a demoralizing effect on
those who are trying to follow the Way of
truth and life. People are very easily
discouraged, and it is easier to live down
to people's expectations than it is to live
up to the moral standards set by God.

But God's attitudes are different from human
attitudes. This great promise about God's
Servant speaks to the needs of ordinary
people. Jesus knew that each little
glimmer of hope needs careful attention.
Gently fanning our faith, hope, and love
into greater heat and light, Jesus
encourages each one of us to better
intentions, and to an effective redirection
of effort.

Lord,
    I believe; help my unbelief!

*Before I was born the Lord called me; from my
birth he has made mention of my name*

(Isa. 49:1).

My son had just learnt about the beginning
of human life, and he commented: 'God
must have loved me a lot, because I am the
one that was born'.

Yes, God has called each one of us, before we
were born, for a special purpose —
to be his child with his name,
and to share his love with others.

*Abba, Father, bless your child today,
and always.
Amen.*

It is too small a thing for you to be my servant to restore the tribes of Jacob and bring back those of Israel I have kept. I will also make you a light for the Gentiles, that you may bring my salvation to the ends of the earth (Isa. 49:6).

Jesus had a purpose in life.

We also have a purpose in life,
   the same purpose.

Jesus put it in these words for us:
   'Therefore go and make disciples of all nations, baptizing them in the name of the Father and of the Son and of the Holy Spirit, teaching them to obey everything I have commanded you. And surely I am with you always, to the very end of the age' (Matt. 28:19,20).

Help me, Lord, to make this my purpose in my life. Amen.

I offered my back to those who beat me, my
cheeks to those who pulled out my beard ...
Because the Sovereign Lord helps me, I will not
be disgraced ... He who vindicates me is near
(Isa. 50:6-8).

We hit our Lord, we spit in his face —
whenever we forget him,
or wrongfully accuse him of evil,
whenever we grievously and thought-
lessly hurt another child of God.

We receive God's forgiveness and vindication
whenever we repent, whenever we turn to
God for forgiveness and life.

Likewise, when people steadfastly refuse
God's love,
and remain unforgiven,
their punishment is a vindication too.

I'm sorry, Lord.
Please forgive me, for the time when ...
Amen.

*We all, like sheep, have gone astray, each of us
has turned to his own way (Isa. 53:6).*

Stubborn, a stiff-necked generation, lost
sheep. Hypocrites, blind guides, white-
washed sepulchres.

This is how people are before God. He knows
that we cannot find our own way to the
best pastures without a shepherd.

We are hopeless without a perfect Shepherd —
so he sent his own Son.

The Shepherd leads us to perfect pastures —
gives us spiritual food for everyday living.

He gives us living water, so that we may never
be thirsty.

He protects us from all injustice, trouble, and
evil.

And he took on the iniquity of us all.

*Lord, help us always to know the Good
Shepherd, and to follow him. Amen.*

He bore the sin of many, and made intercession for the transgressors (Isa. 53:12).

He did it all —
> he suffered the capture, the mock trial on trumped-up charges, a life sentence, scoffing, shame, degradation, pain, bloodshed, and death.

He did it for me, because of what I am and what
> I've done — a sinner without love but needing love.

And he pleads my case, so that
> I am forgiven,
> I go free,
> for ever.

What a relief!

Thank you, Lord Jesus. Amen.

Rejoice with Jerusalem and be glad for her, all you who love her; rejoice greatly with her, all you who mourn over her (Isa. 66:10).

We appreciate the sunshine of spring after a dull and wet winter.

We know peace after there has been a war.

We have satisfaction after we have been hungry.

We experience real joy after a time of sadness.

Jerusalem was in ruins and desolated. When it was rebuilt, there would be a celebration.

Our lives are full of sin, and a mess. But we rejoice, when our sins are forgiven.

So, may we all learn to rejoice.

*My unfailing love for you will not be shaken nor
my covenant of peace be removed, says the Lord,
who has compassion on you (Isa. 54:10).*

Covenants were sealed with blood.
Because there were no written records, an
agreement between two people was
ratified with the shedding of animal blood.
This bound the two people to keeping the
agreement; what happened to the animals
would happen to them if they did not keep
the covenant. There were also witnesses
present to verify what had taken place.

The covenant that God made with us is sealed
with the blood of his own Son.

This covenant of God's unfailing love will —
forgive those who come to him;
destroy those who persist in following
their own whims.

God loves us.

He means it.

Dear God, help us love you. Amen.

*I, even I, am he who blots out your
transgressions, for my own sake, and remembers
your sins no more. Review the past for me, let us
argue the matter together; state the case for your
innocence (Isa. 43:25,26).*

God, the Judge, is demanding that we state
our case.
Do we plead guilty or not guilty?
The people of Israel were guilty — people,
nation, priests — and God punished them
(in exile).
We too have been guilty.

But now God wants to find us not guilty.
He wants to see us go free,
to be forgiven, for ever.

Why? For his own sake,
because Jesus died on the cross.

*Lord Jesus,
we give you our thanks for defending us,
for pleading our case,
and for proving us righteous. Amen.*

The people walking in darkness have seen a great
light; on those living in the land of the shadow of
death a light has dawned (Isa. 9:2).

LIGHT —
    shows the way to go;
    overcomes fears and evil;
    provides a time to work;
    enables us to see everything clearly;
    brings warmth;
    is energy;
    was the first thing created by God;
    is a source of fruitfulness and life;
    is easier to walk toward than away from;
    attracts insects — and people.

Jesus is my LIGHT!

I confess my iniquity; I am troubled by my sin
(Ps. 38:18).

If I had cherished sin in my heart, the Lord would not have listened; but God has surely listened and heard my voice in prayer (Ps. 66:18,19).

We receive God's grace (forgiveness)
    when we are repentant.

We fail to receive his forgiveness when we have
    no sorrow (are not troubled)
    for the wrongs we have done.

Forgiven people confess their sin.
    Unforgiven people cherish it in their heart.

God listens to, and answers, repentant sinners.

God finally turns his back on the unrepentant
    who have turned their back on God.

Praise be to God,
    who has not rejected my prayer or withheld
    his love from me! (Ps. 66:20)

*Because of all my enemies, I am the utter
contempt of my neighbours; I am a dread to my
friends — those who see me on the street flee
from me (Ps. 31:11).*

No one wants to look at a person on a cross.
It is not a pretty sight.
But we have to do it to realize the
seriousness of sin — our sins.

To carry the guilt of our own sins is crippling
and demoralizing.

But to look at Jesus on the cross —
and to leave our sins there —
releases us from this burden and frees us
from sin, guilt, and the power of the devil.

We must learn to accept Jesus on the cross to
gain the benefits of the empty cross.

Lord,
*open my eyes that I may see your
goodness. Amen.*

I call on the Lord in my distress, and he answers me. Save me, O Lord, from lying lips and from deceitful tongues (Ps. 120:1,2).

Jesus said: 'Blessed are you when people insult you, persecute you and falsely say all kinds of evil against you because of me' (Matt. 5:11).

There are times when slander or other persecution is part of our lives. Even when we know why, or deserve it, it still hurts.

The Bible tells us to expect it. Jesus was slandered and persecuted and unjustly accused of blasphemy, and, as his followers, the same will happen to us.

Several psalmists plead their cause before God, stating their innocence and leaving God to vindicate them — they trusted God to punish the wicked and free the innocent.

God, the just Judge, does that by means of the cross of Jesus Christ.

Jesus,
> *people slandered you,*
> *and I receive the blessings.*
> *Thank you. Amen.*

O Lord, do not rebuke me in your anger or discipline me in your wrath. Be merciful to me, Lord, for I am faint; O Lord, heal me, for my bones are in agony. My soul is in anguish. How long, O Lord, how long? Turn, O Lord, and deliver me (Ps. 6:1-4).

We keenly feel it when God judges us —
but he also defends us,
and then takes the sentence upon himself,
to set us free, for ever.

In Psalm 6, David is overcome (perhaps even sick) because of the evil that surrounds him. Realizing that God is the only one to help him, he pleads to God to support him and to deliver him.

Verses 8–10 show that God did answer and that David could stand tall and happy. His enemies would be ashamed and in disgrace.

He would confidently tell evil to 'go away', because God was on his side.

Jesus gives us that same power, to be used when temptation faces us.

God, the Father, Son, and Holy Spirit, deliver me from evil. Amen.

*Why are you downcast, O my soul? Why so
disturbed within me? Put your hope in God, for I
will yet praise him, my Saviour and my God*
(Ps. 43:5).

Happy is the person whose guilt is forgiven.
When I covered up my guilty conscience,
    I felt sick and sorry for myself.
I opened up my heart to God, and stated my
    guilt.
    He forgave me.
Let others pray too, in times of stress.
    God is there with his strength and safety.
Take heart from my experiences.
    I can help others in similar circumstances.
Like a trained animal, keep yourself under
    control.
    Let me help you, too.
The non-believer has many worries,
    but believers are kept safe in God's hand.
Let your happiness show;
    tell others of your new-born joy.
               (Paraphrase of Psalm 32)

O Lord, do not rebuke me in your anger or discipline me in your wrath. For your arrows have pierced me, and your hand has come down upon me (Ps. 38:1,2).

I feel miserable.
   I keep calling to God.
   My friends leave me; my enemies plot against me.
   I can't see, I can't hear, I can't think, I can't speak.

But God, I do know you are there.
   You will answer me.
   I am a sinner. I am guilty.
   God, please help me quickly.

(Summary of Psalm 38)

God, turn our introverted vision into extroverted insight. Amen.

Have mercy on me, O God, according to your
unfailing love; according to your great
compassion blot out my transgressions (Ps. 51:1).

In Psalm 51, David confesses his sin. He
admits that what he did is wrong, and that
it needs not only to be confessed but also
to be forgiven by God. He goes on to ask
God to clean him properly — whiter than
snow. And not just this one sin, but his
whole life, starting from his heart and
working outward.

It is only after this that David can then go out
and help others to come to God and
receive his forgiveness. In response to this
goodness from God, David can sing and
proclaim and write psalms about God's
deliverance.

David writes that it is not outward actions that
God wants, but a repentant heart. God can
mend only a broken heart.

To show that God has worked in him with
forgiveness, love, and pardon, David then
gets on with church-going and sacrifices.

God,
    don't look at my clothes;
    just work on my heart. Amen.

Hear my prayer, O Lord; let my cry for help come to you
(Ps. 102:1).

Psalm 102 is a cry to the Lord:
a cry for help,
pouring out feelings of guilt, worthlessness, and ill health;

a cry for help,
to the God who is in control of the universe, the nations, and us;

a cry for help,
to be recorded for other people,
so that future generations may praise, worship, and acknowledge God;

a cry of pleasure,
for God, the God of creation, of productivity, of protection, STILL LOVES US.

Kingdoms come and kingdoms go,
but you, God, go on for ever. Amen.

*Out of the depths I cry to you, O Lord; O Lord,
hear my voice. Let your ears be attentive to my
cry for mercy (Ps. 130:1,2).*

When we hit rock bottom,
    God picks us up and sets us climbing
      again.
    And he will get us to the top, too.

We will overcome,
    because he has already overcome all evil
    on the cross.

He does not keep a record of what I do;
    rather, he forgives.

Therefore we worship and honour, and trust
    and serve.

Because nothing can shatter our hope.

*Dear God,
    set my feet walking,
    uphill to you. Amen.*

I remember the days of long ago; I meditate on all your works and consider what your hands have done. I spread out my hands to you; my soul thirsts for you like a parched land (Ps. 143:5,6).

David knew that only God could be the answer to his problems. He never contemplated going it alone.

We may try going it alone, or seeking the help of doctors, counsellors, or perhaps other religions.

But it's God alone who delivers us —
with living water for thirsty souls,
with bread and wine for repentant sinners,
with printed words for hungry minds.

God,
for what you have done,
for what your hands have made,
and for the way you continue to sustain us,
we will love you with all our hearts,
and with all our soul,
and with all our might. Amen.

Hosanna! Blessed is he who comes in the name of the Lord! Blessed is the King of Israel!
(John 12:13).

The Messianic Psalms (2,8,16,22,45,69,72, 89,110,132) tell us not only of a triumphant king, but also of a despised and rejected man.

It is amazing in what detail each prophecy was fulfilled. God certainly had a plan, which he revealed to people willing to listen and learn — not from learned scholars, but from a humble carpenter, who is God himself.

God still reveals himself to us today.

May our eyes be opened,
    may our ears be unstopped,
    our legs able to run,
    and our tongues talk of the joy,
    and peace,
    and love,
    and truth. (See Isa. 35:5,6)

Rejoice greatly, O Daughter of Zion! Shout,
Daughter of Jerusalem! See, your king comes to
you, righteous and having salvation, gentle and
riding on a donkey, on a colt, the foal of a donkey
(Zech. 9:9).

O Lord, save us; O Lord, grant us success.
Blessed is he who comes in the name of
the Lord (Ps. 118:25,26).

'Hosanna' means 'save us'. The Jews were
taught that this Psalm (especially these
verses) is the song they would sing as they
escorted their Messiah-King into
Jerusalem when he appeared to them. It
would be a national procession; waving
palm branches was part of their symbolic
acts during the nationalistic Festival of
Tabernacles.

Their kings rode horses into war, and they rode
asses (animals which worked humbly) for
their coronations and at processions and
festivals.

Hosanna to you in the highest, O Lord.

You have cut short the days of his youth; you
have covered him with a mantle of shame
                                    (Ps. 89:45).

Just as Jesus was reaching the prime of life,
    just as he was establishing his career, just
    as people were beginning to listen and
    take notice of his teachings, he was
    crucified.

Crucifixion was used for traitors, for political
    and religious treason, for robbery and
    murder. Only criminals who were non-
    Roman citizens were crucified. (Criminals
    who were Roman citizens were beheaded
    — a less shameful, less painful form of
    execution.)

And it was all for us.

They divide my garments among them and cast lots for my clothing (Ps. 22:18).

The soldiers who were on guard duty at a crucifixion were allowed an extra ration of wine for their personal use (sometimes herbs were added to heighten the effects of the wine and disguise its cheap flavour), and they were given the rights to share the clothes of the condemned person. These extra benefits were in addition to their normal wage, as compensation for the unpleasant task.

According to John's report of this incident (John 19:23), Jesus' robe or tunic was woven in one piece and therefore more valuable left as it was. So the soldiers did not tear it, but 'cast lots' (threw dice or drew straws) to see which soldier kept it as a whole garment. In John's gospel, both parts of the prophecy of the Psalm verse came true.

God's attention to detail leaves nothing undone — including the forgiveness of sins for each individual person.

My God, my God, why have you forsaken me?
Why are you so far from saving me, so far from
the words of my groaning? (Ps. 22:1).

I t's always a lonely job rescuing people.
Having someone to help makes the job
easier! But this was one job Jesus had to
do by himself — all by himself.

That's how important it was;
    how difficult it was;
    how impossible it was;
    how necessary it was.

There wasn't anyone who could do it instead of
    him. And there wasn't anyone who could
    help him — then.

Dear Jesus,
    show me how I can help you now. Amen.

They put gall in my food and gave me vinegar for my thirst (Ps. 69:21).

Wine mingled with gall, or myrrh, was used to dull the pain for the crucified person. Jesus did not want any of this when it was offered to him before he was nailed to the cross (Matthew and Mark) or while he was on the cross (Luke).

The vinegar offered to him when he said 'I am thirsty' (John 19:28) was probably some of the cheap wine which the soldiers had been issued for their own use. Jesus' cry came from a human need just before dying, and showed that his death was imminent and real.

Jesus did not look forward to the pain and death before him. But neither did not shirk any of it. He bore our sin and all the consequences of it fully, to the utmost and without pain-killers. And he did it perfectly.

Let us fix our eyes on Jesus, the author and perfecter of our faith, who for the joy set before him endured the cross, scorning its shame, and sat down at the right hand of the throne of God (Heb. 12:2).

He was assigned a grave with the wicked, and
with the rich in his death, though he had done no
violence, nor was any deceit in his mouth

(Isa. 53:9).

The thieves, one on either side;
the centurion who said 'Certainly this man
was innocent!;
Joseph of Arimathea, the rich man who also
belonged to the Sanhedrin Council;
all these men were connected with Jesus'
death.

What did they do after this encounter with their
Saviour?

The thieves died very soon afterwards.
The centurion, being a Roman, would
have gone back to Rome. Joseph of
Arimathea was only in Jerusalem for the
Passover.

Then what?

How are we going to respond to this encounter
with Jesus?

Why do you look for the living among the dead?
He is not here; he has risen! Remember how he
told you, while he was still with you in Galilee:
'The Son of Man must be delivered into the hands
of sinful men, be crucified and on the third day be
raised again' (Luke 24:5-7)

Hallelujah! — which means 'Praise the
Lord!'
He has risen!
The final seal of God's approval on Jesus'
mission is
the Resurrection.

Jesus is the only prophet in all this world's
history who has risen from the grave. He
now lives for ever and guides his bride, the
church, in 'the way and the truth and the
life' (John 14:6).

Hallelujah! Hallelujah! Hallelujah!

Amen, amen; it shall be so!

Like new-born babies, crave pure spiritual milk,
so that by it you may grow in your salvation, now
that you have tasted that the Lord is good
(1 Peter 2:2,3).

Lent and Easter don't finish on Easter
Sunday —
we keep some Easter eggs for later, and
we have extra holidays, too.

We also have more spiritual living to do —
praising God for the resurrection,
growing in faith and knowledge,
showing it in our living,
talking about what it means for everyday
life,
helping others too to come to Christ,
looking forward to that time when we join
Jesus in heaven.

Easter is not the end. It's a beginning — the
beginning to *life* with God.

Take my life and let it be ... LIFE

[You] crowned him with glory and honour. You
made him ruler over the works of your hands
(Ps. 8:5,6).

Jesus has conquered.

Jesus has power.

Jesus has life.

Jesus rules!

And so do we, through our baptism.

In the name of Jesus, we can do all things — to
bring others to faith in him.

The purpose of Jesus' life and death and resurrection is to save us.

And the purpose of our lives is to share this
salvation with everyone we meet.

O Lord, our Lord,
how majestic is your name in all the earth.

*I know that my Redeemer lives, and that in the
end he will stand upon the earth. And after my
skin has been destroyed, yet in my flesh I will see
God; I myself will see him with my own eyes — I,
and not another. How my heart yearns within me!*
(Job 19:25-27).

The old translations of the last line read:
'My heart faints within me!'

My heart faints sometimes too, when I think of
what God has done for me.

Then I recover enough to get going and do
something to show that I am alive!

Something
— a cup of cold water (or hot coffee);
— a visit to the sick, elderly, or lonely;
— sharing material blessings with the
needy;
— listening to an unresolved problem —
again!
— spending time with children.

Something for Jesus.

He will swallow up death for ever. The Sovereign Lord will wipe away the tears from all faces.

(Isa. 25:8).

If there were no resurrection, there would be no hope, no joy, no God. We would be the most deceived people in the whole of the world's existence.

But the resurrection is a sure thing. It is real — so real as to be 'unreal'!

Because Jesus has been raised from death — so will we.

Death is conquered. It is no longer a threat to our living. We can say to death (and Satan and all forms of evil):
'You have no power over me'.

Death is gone. Therefore, so has sadness, emptiness, and tears.

The Sovereign Lord rules,
and happiness is ours.

O Lord, you are my God; I will exalt you and praise your name, for in perfect faithfulness you have done marvellous things, things planned long ago (Isa. 25:1).

I will sprinkle clean water on you, and you will be clean; I will cleanse you from all your impurities and from all your idols. I will give you a new heart and put a new spirit in you; I will remove from you your heart of stone and give you a heart of flesh. And I will put my Spirit in you and move you to follow my decrees and be careful to keep my laws (Ezek. 36:25-27).

It isn't enough that our houses be clean. They must also be functional with furniture, equipment, and all the things necessary for daily life, such as food and clothes.

It isn't enough that our lives be cleaned up from sin and guilt; there must also be a new direction and incentive for our daily lives.

God's law of love (caring and sharing) is what he places into our lives; he gives us a heart of flesh. Motivated by the Spirit, we move on to living a free, clean, happy, stimulating life for God.

Dear Lord,
fill my heart of flesh with your laws. Amen.

Show me your ways, O Lord, teach me your paths; guide me in your truth and teach me, for you are God my Saviour, and my hope is in you all day long. Good and upright is the Lord; therefore he instructs sinners in his ways. He guides the humble in what is right and teaches them his way (Ps. 25:4,5,8,9).

God doesn't leave us in a vacuum — or, even worse, leave us in this evil world with no help and direction.

Instead, he guides and directs us.

He tells us what is right and what is wrong.

He answers all our questions.

He protects us from danger.

He blesses our work.

But most importantly, he forgives us our sins.

God is good:
>   he makes sure we can be, too, through Jesus, our Saviour.

*Therefore my heart is glad and my tongue
rejoices; my body also will rest secure, because
you will not abandon me to the grave, nor will
you let your Holy One see decay (Ps. 16:9,10).*

Rejoice!

What God has done is worth being happy
about, even having a party with lots of
friends; it calls for 'making a joyful noise'
and 'shouting aloud' (see Psalms 95 and
100).

So let's shout!

That implies that there are people to hear what
we have to say.

In the Judean hills around Jerusalem, one did
not shout or sing or make a joyful noise
just to oneself. Others heard. And it did
not have to be tuneful or professional —
just joyful and loud.

God has done marvellous things — the most
marvellous being to rescue us from
eternal death. Let's tell everyone we meet.

God,
teach me what to say.
And may I say it aloud. Amen.

Shout with joy to God, all the earth! Sing the glory of his name: make his praise glorious! Say to God, 'How awesome are your deeds!'

(Ps. 66:1).

Psalm 66 describes the reactions of the Israelites after they had come through the Red Sea (see Exodus 14 and 15).

The people of Israel were camped beside the sea, and Pharaoh's army was fast approaching. They could see that they were going to die, either by the sword or by drowning.

But God had a different way — life, through the sea.

There is only one reaction when God delivers us —
we shout.
we sing,
we dance.

That's what the people of Israel did.

And so can we!

Lord, may we sing and move to the beat of your drum. Amen.

*Sing to the Lord a new song, for he has done
marvellous things; his right hand and his holy arm
have worked salvation for him. The Lord has
made his salvation known and revealed his
righteousness to the nations (Ps. 98:1,2).*

It's not a secret any longer.
It's not just the same old story.
It's not just for a chosen few.

It's marvellous, wonderful.
It's salvation.
It's for everyone.

Such good news is worthy of a new song.

But how can we compose the music and put
    words to it? Our feeble lives are too small
    to do justice to such a great God.

*Holy Spirit,
    show us what we are to do to sing a new
    song to our Lord. Amen.*

I rejoiced with those who said to me, 'Let us go to the house of the Lord' (Ps. 122:1).

In the company of other believers, we can share our faith and express our happiness together. Together we can sing, praise, and witness. But at the same time, worshipping is still a personal experience — between God and me.

Going through the doors of church is a witness to other believers and to non-believers, too. But once we are through the doors, we are in God's presence, and it's then that God relates to us as individuals. He works on and in our hearts.

It is good to go to church — not to 'show off' our faith, but to get it strengthened.

We then go out to 'show off' the God who has delivered us from sin, death, and hell.

God,
blessed are those who dwell in your house;
they are ever praising you. (Ps. 84:4)

*I will praise God's name in song and glorify him
with thanksgiving. This will please the Lord more
than an ox, more than a bull with its horns and
hoofs (Ps. 69:30,31).*

Sacrifices in the temple were good —
bulls were used by the rich; the poor could
only afford sheep, goats, or doves.

But songs of praise were better —
they involved other people as choir and
listeners.

Not everyone has the talent, though, to write
songs — or to sing them.

But everyone does have a talent that can be
used in some way to tell the Good News of
Jesus Christ:
perhaps a cup of cold water,
a visit in times of need,
help for the handicapped,
encouragement for the depressed,
leading a Bible study,
teaching Sunday-school —
just ordinary sharing and caring in everyday
actions.

We can all praise God's name in some way, and
'glorify him with thanksgiving'.

Come, all you who are thirsty, come to the
waters; and you who have no money, come, buy
and eat! Come, buy wine and milk without money
and without cost (Isa. 55:1).

God invites us to his banquet, even
though we have no worth, no merit of our
own. The food and drink he serves is
wholesome and satisfying.

The people are implored to come to God —
now.
The wicked are to give up their ways, the
evil to give up their plotting and planning.
God will pardon them, freely.

God's ways are not our ways. God's way is the
only way.

Having come to God, we receive forgiveness,
joy, and peace. Now we can go out into the
'daily grind', the 'rat-race', and spread his
good news. God's peace and joy can overcome the hostility and fear that this world
produces. This is for sure.

May my life always reflect the love and forgive-
ness which comes from you, O God,
the Creator,
the Redeemer,
the Sanctifier. Amen.

*Then I heard every creature in heaven and on
earth and under the earth and on the sea, and all
that is in them, singing: 'To him who sits on the
throne and to the Lamb be praise and honour and
glory and power, for ever and ever!' (Rev. 5:13).*

May we add our voices to those praising
God —
God the Father, who made us;
God the Son, who redeemed us;
God the Holy Spirit, who washes us.

'They sang a new song:
"You are worthy to take the scroll and to
open its seals, because you were slain,
and with your blood you purchased men
for God from every tribe and language and
people and nation. You have made them to
be a kingdom and priests to serve our
God, and they will reign on earth."

'Then I looked and heard the voice of many
angels, numbering thousands upon
thousands, and ten thousand times ten
thousand. They encircled the throne and
the living creatures and the elders. In a
loud voice they sang:
"Worthy is the Lamb, who was slain, to
receive power and wealth and wisdom and
strength and honour and glory and
praise!" ' (Rev. 5:9–12)

May the God of peace, who raised from the dead our Lord Jesus Christ, provide you with every good thing you need in order to do his will.